MONEY JOURNEY WE NEED TO EXPLORE

10 fantastic routes to grow financially.

Jeff Stella

Copyright @ 2024 by JEFF STELLA
All rights reserved.

TABLE OF CONTENTS

INTRODUCTION.   EMBARKING ON MONEY JOURNEY.

ROUTE 1.   INVEST IN YOURSELF

ROUTE 2.   SAVE AND BUDGET

ROUTE 3.   SEEK TECHNOLOGY KNOWLEDGE

ROUTE 4.   MASTERING SKILLS TO PERFECTION

ROUTE 5.   NETWORKING AND BUILDING RELATIONSHIPS

ROUTE 6.   DIVERSIFYING YOUR INCOME

ROUTE 7.   EXPLORE DEEPLY

ROUTE 8.   SEEKING FINANCIAL ADVICE

ROUTE 9.   STAY CONSISTENT AND DISCIPLINED

ROUTE 10.   REFLECTION AND CONTINUING THE JOURNEY

INTRODUCTION

EMBARKING ON MONEY JOURNEY

In a world where Financial stability frequently feels like a fugitive dream, embarking on a trip to understand and master the realm of plutocrats becomes not just a desire but a necessity. Drink to" Money Journey Exploring the Path to Fiscal Commission," a companion designed to navigate the intricate geography of particular finance. Within these runners, we embark on transformative Routes, illuminating the frequently daunting world of plutocrat operation with clarity, sapience, and practicable strategies. Whether you are just starting on your fiscal passage or seeking to upgrade your living practices, this book offers a comprehensive roadmap to empower you every step of the way. As we claw into the core principles of budgeting, investing, saving, and aware spending, we'll uncover the secrets to unleashing fiscal freedom and achieving your dreams. From understanding the psychology of money to deciphering the intricacies of market dynamics, this book serves as a beacon of knowledge, empowering you to make informed decisions and chart your course toward a brighter financial future. So, fasten your seatbelt and prepare for an expedition like no other one that promises to enlighten, inspire, and transform your relationship with money forever.

But this trip is not simply about accumulating wealth; it's about fostering a deeper understanding of the part plutocrats play in our lives and employing its power to shape our futures appreciatively. Prepare to embark on a trip of discovery, commission, and enlightenment. Together, let's embark on the plutocrat trip and map a course toward a brighter, more prosperous hereafter.

ROUTE I

INVEST IN YOURSELF:

CONTINUOSLY LEARNING AND DEVELOP YOURSELF

Investing in yourself is like embarking on a particular trip of growth and development. It involves nurturing your heartstrings, expanding your knowledge, and embracing new gest. By prioritizing enhancement, you can unleash your full eventuality and produce a fulfilling life. So do not vacillate to invest in your dreams, explore your interests, and seize openings that align with your values. Flashback is the topmost investment you can make to make perfect growth.

Absolutely! Investing in yourself is like planting seeds for unborn growth and success. One way to do this is by fastening on a particular development. This can involve setting pretensions, perfecting your chops, and expanding your knowledge.

It's also important to take care of your physical and internal well-being. Prioritize care, compass yourself with positive influences, and seek out openings for growth. Investing in yourself is a lifelong trip that pays off in numerous ways, It's all about taking a way to improve and grow in colorful aspects of your life. You can invest in your education by taking courses to learn new abilities. Value and concentrate on your goals.

Investing in yourself is an ongoing process that can lead to particular and professional growth. So, go ahead and make yourself a precedence

In the pursuit of success, amidst the clamor of external openings and challenges, there lies a frequently overlooked investment occasion, one that holds the key to unleashing your full eventuality and achieving your dreams. This investment is in yourself. In this route, we explore the profound impact of investing in yourself and why it's the foundation of particular growth and success. The Power of tone- Investment, Investing in yourself isn't simply a fiscal sale; it's a commitment to your growth and development. It encompasses a wide array of conduct and choices that prioritize your well-being, education, chops, and overall fulfillment. Unlike traditional investments that may change with request conditions, the returns on investment are profound and continuing, shaping not only your external circumstances but also your internal geography. Nonstop Literacy and Skill Development One of the most significant aspects of investing in yourself is the pursuit of knowledge and skill accession. Whether through formal education, online courses, shops, or tone study, the hunt for literacy opens doors to new openings and expands your capabilities. In the moment's fast-paced world, where diligence evolves fleetly and new technologies crop constantly, staying stagnant isn't an option. By investing in nonstop literacy, you equip yourself with the tools demanded to thrive in a dynamic terrain and remain applicable in your field. Cultivating Adaptability and Rigidity Life is changeable, filled with both triumphs and lapses. Investing in yourself fosters adaptability and rigidity the capability to bounce back from adversity and thrive in the face of change. Through tone-reflection, awareness practices, and particular development sweats, you strengthen your inner adaptability, enabling you to navigate challenges with grace and crop stronger on the other side. By embracing change as an occasion for growth rather than trouble, you place yourself as a redoubtable force capable of riding any storm. Prioritizing Health and Well-being True success encompasses further than just professional achievements; it encompasses holistic well-being, physical, internal, and emotional. Investing in yourself means prioritizing tone- care, maintaining a balanced life, and nurturing healthy habits. Whether it's through regular exercise, proper nutrition, acceptable rest, or seeking support when demanded, taking care of your well-being lays the foundation for sustained success and happiness. Flashback, you can not pour from an empty mug; prioritizing tone care isn't selfish but essential for long-term flourishing. Fostering Confidence and Tolerance Believing in yourself is important to achieving your pretensions and bournes.

Investing in yourself cultivates confidence and efficacy, the belief in your capability to succeed in specific situations or negotiate tasks. As you acquire new chops, overcome challenges, and see palpable progress in your trials, your confidence grows, propelling you forward with unwavering determination. This assurance becomes a catalyst for success, empowering you to take advised pitfalls, seize openings, and chart your path with conviction. Conclusion In the trip of life, there's no lesser investment than the bone you make in yourself. By prioritizing nonstop literacy, cultivating adaptability, nurturing your well-being, and fostering confidence, you lay the root for particular growth and success. Flashback, the tips of investment are bottomless, empowering you to produce a life filled with purpose, fulfillment, and measureless possibilities. So, dare to invest bravely in yourself, for it's the ultimate investment with the loftiest returns.

ROUTE II

SAVE AND BUDGET:

Mastering the Art of Saving and Budgeting, Builds a Strong Financial Foundation

The trip toward fiscal stability and security, saving and budgeting are the keystones upon which a solid foundation is erected. Whether your pretensions are short-term or long-term, having a robust savings plan and an effective budgeting strategy can pave the way for achieving your bournes and riding unanticipated fiscal storms. The significance of Saving isn't simply setting aside plutocrats for a stormy day; it's a mindset and a crucial element of fiscal well-being. Then are some reasons why saving is pivotal Emergency Fund Life is changeable, and extremities can arise at any moment as unforeseen medical expenditure, auto repairs, or unanticipated job loss. An exigency fund serves as a safety net, furnishing fiscal security during tough times without resorting to debt. Achieving pretensions Whether it's buying a house, going on a dream holiday, or retiring comfortably, saving is essential for turning bournes into reality. Setting specific, measurable pretensions helps motivate harmonious saving habits. Financial Freedom Saving diligently enables you to break free from stipend-to-stipend living and achieve fiscal independence. With sufficient savings, you have further inflexibility to pursue openings, change careers, or retire beforehand. Strategies for Effective Saving require discipline and planning. Then are some strategies to help you save more effectively Pay Yourself First Treat saving as a non-negotiable expenditure. Allocate a portion of your income toward savings before covering other charges. Automate Savings Set up automatic transfers from your checking account to your savings regard. This removes the temptation to spend plutocrats allocated for savings. Track Charges Cover your spending habits to identify areas where you can cut back and deflect finances toward savings pretensions. Start Small, Increase Over Time If saving seems daunting, start with a manageable quantum and gradationally increase it as your income grows or charges drop. Take Advantage of Windfalls Direct unanticipated felicities, similar to duty refunds or lagniappes, toward savings rather than splurging on optional purchases. The Power of Budgeting is the design for managing your finances effectively. It provides clarity on where your plutocrat is coming from, where it's going, and how you can allocate it wisely. Then why budgeting is necessary for fiscal mindfulness? A budget helps you understand your income and charges, empowering you to make informed opinions about your finances. Expense Control By tracking your spending, you can identify gratuitous charges and prioritize essential bones, ensuring that your plutocrat is allocated efficiently. Debt Management Budgeting allows you to allocate finances toward debt prepayment totally, accelerating your trip toward fiscal freedom. thing Alignment A budget aligns your spending with your fiscal pretensions, make sure you are making progress toward what matters most to you. Creating an Effective

Budget Casting a budget involves assessing your fiscal situation, setting realistic pretensions, and allocating coffers consequently. Follow this way to produce an effective budget Calculate Income Determine your total yearly income from all sources. List Charges Make a comprehensive list of all your charges, including fixed (e.g., rent, serviceability) and variable(e.g., groceries, entertainment). separate Needs, and Differentiate between essential charges necessary for survival and optional spending on unnecessary particulars. Set Precedences Allocate finances toward high-precedence particulars similar to debt prepayment, savings, and essential charges before optional spending. Track Progress Regularly cover your spending against your budget to identify diversions and acclimate as necessary. acclimatize and Evolve Life circumstances and fiscal precedences may change over time. Readdress and revise your budget periodically to reflect these changes.

In conclusion, saving and budgeting aren't restrictive measures but empowering tools that give fiscal freedom and peace of mind. By cultivating saving habits and clinging to a well-allowed budget, you can navigate fiscal challenges, achieve your pretensions, and make a secure future for yourself and your loved ones

ROUTE III

SEEK TECHNOLOGY KNOWLEDGE:

The Quest for Technological Knowledge

In the ever-evolving geography of technology, the hunt for knowledge is akin to embarking on a trip through a vast, uncharted home. It's a trip filled with excitement, challenges, and endless possibilities. For numerous, the pursuit of technological knowledge isn't simply a task but a passion. A grim drive to understand, introduce, and produce.
The trip begins with a spark and inextinguishable curiosity that ignites the desire to claw deeper into the realm of technology. It could be a seductiveness with computers, a curiosity about artificial intelligence, or a desire to unravel the mystifications of rendering languages. Whatever the provocation, it's this original curiosity that propels individuals forward, prompting them to seek out the knowledge that lies beyond. Crossing the Threshold With determination in their hearts, aspiring technologists embark on their hunt, crossing the threshold from the familiar into the unknown. They enter a world of endless possibilities, where every discovery leads to new questions and every challenge presents an occasion for growth. It's a world where the only limits are those of one's imagination and perseverance. The Road of Trials Along the road of trials, aspiring technologists encounter obstacles and lapses that test their resoluteness. From scuffling with complex algorithms to troubleshooting bugs in law, each challenge presents an occasion to learn and ameliorate. It's through perseverance and determination that they overcome these obstacles, arising stronger and more knowledgeable than ahead. Meeting Instructors and Abettors On their trip, aspiring technologists frequently find instructors and abettors who guide and support them

along the way. Whether through online forums, rendering communities, or mentorship programs, these individualities give inestimable perceptivity, advice, and stimulants. They partake in their knowledge and gests, helping to light the path forward for those who follow in their steps. Embracing Innovation and Creativity As the trip unfolds, aspiring technologists learn to embrace invention and creativity. They explore new ideas, trial with arising technologies, and push the boundaries of what's possible. It's through their creativity and imagination that they make improvements, solve problems and drive progress in the world of technology. The Ultimate Price Eventually, the hunt for technological knowledge is its own. With each new skill learned, each challenge overcome, and each invention realized, aspiring technologists find fulfillment in their trip. Whether they're erecting software, designing tackle, or exploring the borders of technology, they're driven by a passion for knowledge and a desire to make a difference in the world. Conclusion The hunt for technological knowledge is a trip of discovery, growth, and endless possibilities. It's a trip that begins with curiosity and determination and leads to invention and fulfillment. Along the way, aspiring technologists encounter challenges, lapses, and instructors who help guide them on their path. In the end, they crop stronger, wiser, and ready to continue pushing the boundaries of what's possible in the world of technology, so do more and find technology knowledge.

ROUTE IV

Mastering Skills to Perfection

In the pursuit of excellence, mastering chops to perfection is a trip marked by fidelity, practice, and nonstop refinement. Whether it's learning a musical instrument, honing athletic capacities, or learning a craft, the path to perfection requires a deliberate approach and unvarying commitment. In this route, we'll explore the crucial principles and strategies for determining chops to perfection.

1. **Define Your ideal:** Before embarking on the trip to mastery, it's essential to define your objective easily. What skill do you want to perfect? What position of proficiency do you aim to achieve? Setting specific, measurable pretensions provides clarity and direction, guiding your sweats towards mastery.

2. **Embrace Deliberate Practice:** At the core of skill mastery lies deliberate practice. Chased by psychologist Anders Ericsson, deliberate practice involves engaging in focused, purposeful

training to perfect performance. It's not simply going through the movements but rather pushing beyond your comfort zone, relating sins, and addressing them through targeted practice.

3. **Cultivate Discipline and Tolerance:** learning a skill to perfection demands discipline and tolerance. It's a long-term bid that requires harmonious trouble and adaptability in the face of lapses. Stay married to your practice routine, indeed when progress seems slow, and trust in the incremental earnings accumulated over time.

4. **Seek Feedback and Guidance:** Feedback is inestimable on the trip to mastery. Seek guidance from instructors, trainers, or peers who can offer formative review and perceptivity to help upgrade your fashion. Embrace feedback as an occasion for growth, incorporating it into your practice to continually elevate your performance.

5. **dissect and Reflect:** Reflection is an important tool for skill development. Take time to dissect your practice sessions and performances critically. What went well? What areas need

enhancement? By relating strengths and sins, you can confirm your practice approach to address specific areas for growth effectively.

6. **Embrace Challenges and Push Limits:** True mastery is forged through prostrating challenges and pushing the limits of your capacities. Do not wince down from delicate tasks or lapses; rather, view them as openings to stretch your chops and expand your capabilities. Embrace the discomfort of growth, knowing that it's through prostrating challenges that you will eventually achieve mastery.

7. **Foster a Growth Mindset:** Cultivate a growth mindset, believing that capacities can be developed through fidelity and hard work. Embrace miscalculations as learning openings and view obstacles as stepping monuments on the path to mastery. By espousing a mindset concentrated on growth and adaptability, you will navigate the ineluctable ups and campo of skill development with perseverance and sanguinity. Conclusion Mastering chops to perfection is a pursuit fueled by passion, continuity, and a

commitment to nonstop enhancement. By embracing deliberate practice, seeking feedback, and fostering a growth mindset, you can embark on a trip of mastery that leads to unequaled excellence in your chosen trials. Mastery isn't a destination but a lifelong trip of growth and advancement.

ROUTE V

NETWORKING AND BUILDING RELATIONSHIPS

Networking and erecting connections are abecedarian chops that can greatly impact your particular and professional success. In this chapter, we'll look into the significance of networking, strategies for effective networking, and tips for nurturing and maintaining connections.

1. ***The significance of Networking:*** Networking is more than just swapping business cards or connecting on social media; it's about cultivating meaningful connections that can profit you tête-à-tête and professionally. This is why networking is essential, openings Networking opens doors to new openings, whether it's landing a job, chancing a tutor, or discovering implicit collaborators for systems. Knowledge participating Through networking, you can learn from others' gests, gain

perceptivity into different diligence or fields, and stay streamlined on assiduity trends. Support System erecting a strong network provides you with a support system of like-inclined individuals who can offer advice, stimulants, and coffers when demanded. Visibility and Credibility Networking helps you establish your presence and credibility within your assiduity or community, making you more visible to implicit employers, guests, or collaborators.

2. ***Strategies for Effective Networking:*** Effective networking involves both online and offline relations and requires a visionary approach. Consider the following strategies to enhance your networking sweats, Determine what you hope to achieve through networking, whether it's expanding your customer base, advancing your career, or gaining assiduity knowledge. Identify Target Networks Identify applicable networking openings, similar to assiduity events, professional associations, alumni groups, or online forums, where you are likely to meet individuals who partake in your interests or

pretensions. Be Genuine and Authentic Approach networking with a genuine interest in erecting connections rather than solely fastening on what you can gain. Authenticity fosters trust and fellowship with others. hear and Learn Practice active listening when engaging with others. Show genuine interest in their stories, gestures, and perspectives. Networking is as important about learning from others as it's about participating in your perceptivity. Follow-Up After making original connections, follow up with individualities you've met. shoot substantiated dispatches expressing your appreciation for their time and interest in staying connected. Offer Value Look for ways to add value to your network by participating in applicable papers, making prolusions, or offering backing grounded on your chops and moxie.

3. *Nurturing and Maintaining connections*: structure connections are an ongoing process that requires nurturing and conservation. Then are some tips for cultivating strong connections Stay Connected Regularly, reach out to your network through emails, phone calls, or

in-person meetings. harmonious communication helps maintain fellowship and keeps you top of your mind. Be Reliable and Trustworthy Build trust with your network by being dependable, keeping your commitments, and following through on pledges. Show Gratitude Express gratefulness to your connections for their support, advice, or backing. A simple thank you can go a long way in strengthening connections. Be a Resource Offer your moxie, coffers, or connections to help others in your network achieve their pretensions. liberality fosters reciprocity and strengthens bonds. Celebrate Successes Celebrate mileposts, achievements, and successes with your network. Feting and supporting each other's accomplishments strengthens fellowship and fosters a sense of community.

4. *Networking and erecting connections* are essential chops for particular and professional growth. By laboriously engaging with others, cultivating meaningful connections, and nurturing connections over time, you can expand your openings, gain precious perceptivity, and produce a probative network that enhances your success and well-

being. Flashback that networking isn't just about what you can gain, but also about what you can contribute to others and the community as a whole

ROUTE VI

DIVERSIFYING YOUR INCOME

In a moment's dynamic profitable geography, counting solely on a single source of income is akin to walking a tightrope without a safety net. profitable misgivings, job request oscillations, and unanticipated charges can fluently disrupt fiscal stability. To guard against similar pitfalls, diversifying your income isn't just a prudent choice but a strategic imperative. Understanding Diversification, Diversification involves spreading your income aqueducts across colorful sources, reducing reliance on any single bone
. This principle is akin to the word," Do not put all your eggs in one handbasket." By diversifying, you alleviate the impact of a downturn in one area while potentially saving from growth in another.

Why Diversify Your Income? threat Mitigation Diversification acts as a guard against unlooked-for events similar to job loss, request downturns, or assiduity-specific challenges. However, others can compensate, maintaining fiscal stability, If one income sluice falters. Increased Stability With multiple income aqueducts, you are less vulnerable to oscillations in any particular request or sector. This stability provides peace of mind and allows for further flexible fiscal planning. Enhanced Growth Implicit, Different income sources offer openings for exponential growth. While some gamblers may yield modest returns, others may flourish suddenly, boosting overall earnings. Inflexibility and Freedom Multiple-income aqueducts can have lesser inflexibility in career choices and life opinions. Whether pursuing entrepreneurial trials, freelance systems, or unresistant income aqueducts, diversification subventions the freedom to explore different openings. Strategies for Diversification Explore Side scams Engage in part-time trials or side businesses aligned with your chops, interests, and request demand. This could include freelance work, consulting, training, or e-commerce gambles. Invest Wisely Allocate finances across different investment vehicles such as stocks, bonds, real estate, and collective finances. Consider both traditional and indispensable investments to spread threats and optimize returns. Develop Passive Income Aqueducts that produce sources of unresistant income that induce profit with minimum ongoing trouble. exemplifications include rental parcels, tips from investments, royalties from intellectual property, or chapter marketing. Monetize Your Chops subsidize your moxie by offering online courses, writing books, or furnishing coaching and mentoring services. influence digital platforms to reach global followership and maximize earning implicit. Cultivate Multiple profit Aqueducts Explore avenues for generating income beyond traditional employment. This could involve monetizing pursuits, renting out means, or sharing in the gig frugality through platforms like Uber, Airbnb, or TaskRabbit. Diversifying your income isn't just a fiscal strategy; it's a mindset shift toward adaptability and rigidity. By embracing the principle of diversification, you guard your fiscal future, unlock growth openings, and gain lesser control over your livelihood. Start the moment by exploring new income aqueducts, investing wisely, and cultivating a portfolio that empowers you to thrive in any profitable climate.

ROUTE VII

EXPLORE DEEPLY:

Delving Deep into the Pursuit of Wealth

In the grand shade of mortal trials, many hobbies allure the imagination and drive individualities forward as fervently as the hunt for wealth. plutocrat, in its colorful forms, holds the pledge of security, power, and freedom. Yet, the path to fiscal cornucopia is as intricate as it's charming, taking a mix of strategy, continuity, and imagination. Understanding the Nature of Wealth Define Wealth extends beyond bare currency; it encompasses means, coffers, and openings. Understanding this multifaceted nature is pivotal in navigating the trip towards fiscal substance. Cerebral Dynamics Explore the cerebral underpinnings of wealth accession, including provocations, stations towards plutocrat, and the impact of societal morals and artistic factors. Strategies for Accumulating Wealth Entrepreneurship Embarking on entrepreneurial gambles offers the eventuality for substantial returns. Claw into the principles of relating request requirements, creating value, and scaling businesses for sustainable growth. Investment Learn the art of investment across colorful asset classes, including stocks, real estate, and cryptocurrencies. Understand threat operation, diversification, and the significance of informed decision- timber. Career Advancement Maximize earning implicit through strategic career moves, skill development, and concession ways. Explore avenues for professional growth and using moxie in high- demand fields. Cultivating fiscal knowledge Budgeting and Financial Planning Develop practical chops in budgeting, saving, and long- term fiscal planning. Embrace tools and fabrics for managing income, charges, and investments effectively. Debt operation Navigate the complications of debt, distinguishing between' good' and' bad' debt, and employing strategies to minimize interest payments and optimize fiscal health. nonstop literacy Commit to lifelong literacy in fiscal knowledge, staying abreast of request trends, nonsupervisory changes, and arising openings. Engage with experts, literature, and educational coffers to expand fiscal wit. employing the Power of Networks and connections, Networking Cultivate a different network of connections, instructors, and collaborators to pierce openings, knowledge, and support. utilize the collaborative wisdom and coffers of like- inclined individualities and communities. Collaboration and hookups Explore cooperative gambles, common gambles, and strategic hookups to influence reciprocal strengths and accelerate wealth structure enterprise. prostrating Challenges and Adversity Adaptability Grasp lapses and failures as learning openings, cultivating adaptability and rigidity in the face of adversity. Develop managing mechanisms and mindset strategies to navigate the ineluctable challenges along the trip. Ethics and Integrity Uphold ethical principles and integrity in all fiscal dealings, feting the significance of trust and character in erecting enduring wealth.

In the pursuit of wealth, success isn't solely measured by fiscal criteria but by the fulfillment of one's bournes and benefactions to society. By embarking on this trip with industriousness, foresight, and a commitment to nonstop growth, individualities can navigate the complications of wealth accession and realize their bournes for substance and cornucopia.

ROUTE VIII

SEEKING FINANCIAL ADVICE

When navigating the complex world of particular finance, seeking professional advice can be inestimable. Whether you are planning for withdrawal, investing in the stock request, or managing debt, the guidance of a fiscal counsel can help you make informed opinions and achieve your fiscal pretensions with confidence. In this route, we'll explore the significance of seeking fiscal advice, how to find the right counsel, and what to anticipate from the premonitory process.

1. Why Seek Fiscal Advice? fiscal opinions have long-term counteraccusations on your fiscal well-being. Seeking advice from a fiscal counsel can give you with Expertise Financial counsels have specialized knowledge and experience in colorful areas of finance, including investments, taxation, insurance, and withdrawal planning. Ideal perspective counsels can offer an unprejudiced standpoint, helping you see the bigger picture and avoid emotional decision-

timber. tailored results They can conform fiscal strategies to your specific pretensions, threat forbearance, and fiscal situation. Financial Education Advisors can educate you about fiscal generalities, investment options, and strategies to make wealth over time.

2. Chancing the Right Financial Advisor, Choosing the right fiscal counsel is pivotal for your fiscal success. Consider the following factors when opting an counsel Credentials and Qualifications Look for counsels who hold applicable instruments similar a Certified Financial Planner or Personal Financial Specialist. Fiduciary Duty ensures the counsel is bound by a fiduciary duty to act in your stylish interest at all times, rather than simply recommending products that profit them. Character and Track Record Research the counsel's character, read customer reviews and ask for referrals from musketeers or family. Communication Style Choose a counsel who communicates easily and listens to your enterprises, preferences, and pretensions. figure Structure Understand how the counsel is compensated whether through freights, commissions, or a combination of both and insure it aligns with your preferences.

3. The Advisory Process Once you've named a fiscal counsel, the premonitory process generally involves the following way original Consultation You will meet with the counsel to bandy your fiscal pretensions, enterprises, and current fiscal situation. fiscal Analysis The counsel will gather information about your income, charges, means, arrears, and threat forbearance to assess your fiscal health. thing Setting Together, you will establish short-term and long- term fiscal pretensions, similar to withdrawal planning, saving for education, or copping

a home. Financial Plan Development The counsel will produce a substantiated fiscal plan outlining recommendations for investments, insurance, duty strategies, and estate planning. perpetration Once you authorize the fiscal plan, the counsel will help you apply the recommended strategies, similar to opening investment accounts or copping

insurance programs. Monitoring and Review Your counsel will regularly review your fiscal plan, cover your progress towards your pretensions, and make adaptations as demanded grounded on changes in your life or the fiscal geography.

4. Seeking fiscal advice is a visionary step towards securing your fiscal future. By working with good counsel, you can gain clarity, confidence, and peace of mind knowing that you are making informed opinions aligned with your pretensions. Flashback to stay laboriously engaged in the premonitory process, ask questions, and regularly review your fiscal plan to ensure it continues to meet your evolving requirements.

ROUTE IX

STAY CONSISTENT AND DISCIPLINED:

The power of consistency and discipline

In the trip towards achieving our pretensions and living a fulfilling life, consistency and discipline stand as unvarying pillars. They're the guiding forces that propel us forward when provocation wanes and challenges arise. In this route, we will explore the profound impact of **consistency** and **discipline** on particular growth and success.

1. *Understanding consistency:* consistency is the grim commitment to showing up and putting in the work, day in and day out, anyhow of circumstances or external factors. It's the steady drip of trouble that ultimately carves mountains and achieves greatness. Consistency

types instigation, turning small conduct into habits and habits into achievements.

2. ***The Habit Loop At the core of consistency lies the habit circle,*** a neurological pattern that governs our actions. It consists of a intimation routine, and price. By relating the intimation that spark asked actions, establishing harmonious routines, and satisfying ourselves for staying on track, we can support positive habits and make consistency a natural part of our lives.

3. ***Cultivating Discipline:*** Discipline is the ground between pretensions and accomplishments. It's the capability to stay focused and cleave to a destined course of action, indeed in the face of distractions or temptations. Discipline requires control, determination, and a amenability to immolate short- term pleasures for long- term earnings.

4. ***Erecting a Foundation,*** consistency and discipline are erected upon a foundation of clarity and purpose. By defining our pretensions with clarity and aligning them with our values and heartstrings, we can

cultivate a sense of purpose that energies our commitment and adaptability. When our conduct are driven by a deeper purpose, staying harmonious and disciplined becomes not just a choice, but a calling.

5. **Prostrating Obstacles:** The path to consistency and discipline isn't without its obstacles. There will be days when provocation wanes, lapses do, and dubieties creep in. During these times, it's pivotal to calculate on strategies similar as visualization, positive talk, and responsibility to stay on track. By reframing challenges as openings for growth and literacy, we can turn obstacles into stepping monuments towards our pretensions.

6. **Celebrating Progress,** As we strive for consistency and discipline, it's important to celebrate our progress along the way. Whether it's reaching a corner, learning a new skill, or simply staying true to our commitments, every small palm deserves recognition. By admitting our achievements, we support positive actions and cultivate a sense of accomplishment that energies farther progress.

7. ***Embracing fault Eventually,*** it's essential to embrace fault on the trip towards consistency and discipline. We're bound to stumble and fall along the way, but it's through our miscalculations and failures that we learn, grow, and eventually succeed. By espousing a growth mindset and viewing lapses as openings for growth, we can persist in the face of adversity and continue moving forward towards our pretensions.

Consistency and Discipline aren't simply habits to be cultivated, but merits to be embraced. By committing to showing up each day, staying concentrated on our pretensions, and persisting in the face of challenges, we can unleash our full eventuality and produce the life we fantasize. So let us embrace the power of **consistency** and **discipline**, for it's through these merits that we truly flourish.

ROUTE X

Reflection and Continuing the Journey

As we embark on the tenth route of our plutocrat trip, it's pivotal to break and reflect on the ground covered therefore far. Our disquisition into fiscal knowledge and commission has been transformative, illuminating colorful aspects of particular finance and wealth operation. still, our trip is far from over; there are still uncharted homes to explore and precious assignments to learn. Reflecting on Progress Take a moment to reflect on your particular growth and fiscal perceptivity gained throughout this trip. Consider the following questions What have I learned about plutocrat operation and wealth creation? How have my stations and beliefs about plutocrat evolved? What fiscal habits have I espoused or changed for the better? What difficulties have I faced, and how have I overcome them? What are my fiscal pretensions, and how have they shifted over time? By admitting your progress and understanding your trip's impact, you can more prepare for the road ahead. Embracing nonstop literacy Our disquisition of plutocrat matters is an ongoing process, and there is always further to discover.

As we continue our trip, let's commit to lifelong literacy and growth in the ensuing areas Investment Strategies Claw deeper into investment openings, similar as stocks, bonds, real estate, and indispensable means. Understand threat operation and diversification to make a robust investment portfolio. Financial Planning Develop comprehensive fiscal plans acclimatized to your pretensions, including withdrawal planning, education backing, estate planning, and threat operation. Consider working with a fiscal counsel to navigate complex fiscal opinions. Income Generation Explore avenues for adding your income, whether through career advancement, entrepreneurship, unresistant income aqueducts, or side hustles. Continuously seek openings to enhance your earning eventuality. Financial Wellness Prioritize your overall fiscal well-being by fastening on budgeting, saving, debt operation, and exigency preparedness. Cultivate healthy fiscal habits that contribute to long-term stability and adaptability. Philanthropy and Giving Explore the impact of charitable paying and consider incorporating philanthropy into your fiscal plan. Discover ways to support causes and associations aligned with your values and bournes . Navigating Challenges and Celebrating mileposts Along our trip, we are likely to encounter obstacles and lapses. Whether it's request volatility, unanticipated charges, or particular challenges, adaptability is crucial. Flash back to Stay Flexible Adapt to changing circumstances and acclimate your fiscal plan as demanded. Seek Support spare on trusted instructors, musketeers, and fiscal professionals for guidance and stimulant during grueling times. Celebrate Successes Admit and celebrate mileposts along the way, no matter how small. Fete the progress you've made and use it as provocation to keep moving forward.

Conclusion, The Journey Continues As we conclude this reflection on our plutocrat trip, let's embrace the occasion to continue learning, growing, and evolving on our path to fiscal commission. By staying curious, flexible, and visionary, we can navigate the complications of particular finance with confidence and clarity. The road ahead may be uncertain, but with determination and perseverance, we can produce a brighter fiscal future for ourselves and generations to come.

www.ingramcontent.com/pod-product-compliance
Lightning Source LLC
Chambersburg PA
CBHW050248230526
45470CB00005B/2161